Thank you Fishko for everything, especially for your inspiration and help on pages 2,3,4,5,6,7,8,9,10,11, 12,13,14,15,16,17,18,19,20,21,22,23,24,25,26,27, 28,29,30,31,32,33,34,35,36,37,38,39,40,41,42,43, 44,45,46,47,48,49,50,51,52,53,54,55,56,57,58,59, 60,61,62,63,64,65,66,67,68,69,70,71,72,73,74,75, 76,77,78,79,80,81,82,83,84,85,86,87,88,89,90,91, 92,93,94,95,96,97,98,99,100,101,102,103,104,105, 106,107,108,109,110,111,112,113,114,115,116, 117,118,119,120,121,122,123,124,125,126,127, 128,129,130,131,132,133,134,135,136,137, 138, 139,140,141,142,143,144,145,146,147,148,149, 150,151,152,153,154,155,156,157,158,159 and 160.

I try and make every job that I do

2

Logo: Dancin', a musical.

Illustration of two left feet for article on learning to dance.

that I have ever done before.

4

That's my way of making graphic design difficult.

Graphic design made difficult   Bob Gill

VNR VAN NOSTRAND REINHOLD
_____ New York

Library of Congress Catalog Card Number 91-43193
ISBN 0-442-01098-2

Manufactured in the United States of America

Published by Van Nostrand Reinhold
115 Fifth Avenue
New York, New York 10003

Chapman and Hall
2-6 Boundary Row
London, SE1 8HN, England

Thomas Nelson Australia
102 Dodds Street
South Melbourne 3205
Victoria, Australia

Nelson Canada
1120 Birchmount Road
Scarborough, Ontario M1K 5G4, Canada

16   15   14   13   12   11   10 9   8   7   6   5   4   3   2   1

Library of Congress Cataloging-in-Publication Data
Gill, Bob, 1931–
    Graphic design made difficult / Bob Gill.
        p.   cm.
    Includes index.
    ISBN 0-442-01098-2
    1. Graphic arts—Technique.   I. Title.
NC845.G56   1992
741.6—dc20   91-43193
                        CIP

Contents

1 The problem is the problem

This book is about ordinary graphic problems and how the problems themselves can lead to surprising, original graphic solutions, provided the designer is prepared to let go of any preconceptions about how design is supposed to look.

The first time I practiced what this book is preaching was when I was asked to design a title card for the television sitcom, *Private Secretary,* about an inept secretary.

I wanted to do something that was original. But I kept thinking of ideas based on images I had already seen. Then I realized that my ideas *had* to be based on previous experiences. What else could possibly be in my consciousness but previous experiences?

I would have to go outside of my head to look for an original idea. I decided that getting involved in the new problem was the most likely way of going outside; of having a new experience.

If I could express the uniqueness of what the problem was trying to communicate with an image which was valid *only* for that problem, then I could invent a unique image.

In other words, defining a unique problem should inspire a unique solution.

I redefined the problem, emphasizing that part of the problem which communicated something that was unique.

How can an image which says one thing (private secretary) also say something else (that she's inept) without actually saying it?

Now, at least, I had a unique problem.

I did some research. I visited offices. I watched secretaries. I decided that the most appropriate (inevitable) way to say private secretary was to type it.

private

secretary

The next thing was to suggest that the secretary was inept. I discovered how to do that by watching secretaries make mistakes, and then correct them.

pxixct

private

secreatary

The last thing was to put the rest of the information on the title card. I tried to make it look like a secretary's solution. (A layout done by someone who hadn't studied layout.)

pxixct

private

secreatary

. . . .

CBS televitsiokn

Private Secretary pleased me more than any other job
I had done up until that time because the result looked
inevitable and easy.

It communicated precisely what it was supposed to
communicate : that it was a comedy about an inept
secretary. It was also my first original image.

Up until that time, I, along with most other graphic
designers, was preoccupied with aesthetics and fashion.
We weren't really interested in the problem or
communication. We presumed to know what a well-
designed job should look like, before we bothered to find
out the purpose of the design.

After *Private Secretary,* design, for me, was no longer a
fashionable typeface or a modern layout looking like a
Mondrian with lots of white space. Design became a
process for solving communication problems. Any design
decision was valid as long as it solved the communication
problem in a precise and interesting way.

And as I began thinking in this new way, my relationship
with clients began to change. I stopped trying to ram
my aesthetic prejudices down their throats. Why should
clients have my tastes? My background is in art. Theirs is
in commerce.

We began to communicate on a different level. We talked
about solutions and ideas instead of design.

Of course, the design process doesn't end with getting a
valid idea. It only begins there. The idea has to be
realized. The design decisions must not look arbitrary.
They should look inevitable. They should do justice to the
idea. They should *solve* the problem.

14

Here's another example of how concentrating on the problem, rather than on design, can suggest an interesting, original solution.

Problem:
logo for a series of debates on controversial subjects.

I began logically enough. I tried to *illustrate* a debate. Silhouettes seemed appropriate.

The image communicated. But it was not unique.

Then I realized that the unique quality of debate is not the individual debater, but the clash of argument in the space *between* the debaters.

And, finally, I chose a color likely to do justice to the heat of the situation.

But what if the problem makes a statement which is so ordinary, so boring, that it is not likely to interest anyone?

Taking problems which don't make interesting (unique) statements and redefining them so that they do, it what my graphic design is about. It's how I get my ideas. And images. From the problems themselves.

Before the design process can begin, the original, boring problem should be redefined, so that it makes an interesting statement.

Here's a typical, commercial, ordinary problem:

Design a monogram/logo for Television Automation, a video production company.

Designing a TA is not an interesting problem. It is not likely to inspire an interesting solution. Nor is GM, for General Motors, or GE, for General Electric, or any one of thousands of other company monograms. The problem has to be redefined so that it says something unique.

Original problem:
Monogram/logo for Television Automation.

Redefined:
How can the initials "TA" also say "TV"?

That's better, isn't it?

Now that the problem has been changed into a unique statement, a unique solution should come reasonably quickly:

Take a statement like: we cure cancer free. It isn't
necessary to make a statement like that look interesting.
It *is* interesting. Because it is important.

If you try to make an interesting statement look
interesting, the way it looks, competes with the
statement. The look doesn't make it easier to see,
it makes it harder.

This section has copy which is sufficiently important or
amusing so as not to need additional interest from
unusual typography, or layout, or other graphic tricks.

I deliberately made the design elements boring, so that
they wouldn't compete with the words. There are
thousands of images competing with your design for your
audience's attention. If and when your audience gets
around to yours, make sure that the elements within your
design don't compete with each other.

Original problem:
party invitation which requests guests to bring a bottle.

Redefined:
party invitation which *blackmails* guests into bringing
a bottle.

18

Dear friends:

**John Cole invites you to
a party on Sat. Sept. 9
at 8.30pm at 122 Regents
Park Rd. NW1 Flat D.
RSVP Gro2291
Please bring a bottle.**

Free loaders:

**John Cole invites you to
a party on Sat. Sept. 9
at 8.30pm at 122 Regents
Park Rd. NW1 Flat D.
RSVP Gro2291**

Original problem:
ad announcing a Hollywood ''big deal''.

Redefined:
ad which shows actual deal.

If the foregoing correctly sets forth our understanding,
please sign below the words "AGREED TO," in which case this
shall be deemed a binding agreement between us.

                                   Very truly yours,
                                   THE DINO DELAURENTIIS CORPORATION

                                   By_____

AGREED TO: Dino De Laurentiis

_____
Werner Herzog

**Dino DeLaurentiis proudly announces that Werner Herzog will
direct "Aztec" based on the best-selling novel by Gary Jennnings.**

Original problem:
cover for a booklet which lists the terms of a car rental company.

Redefined:
cover for a booklet which makes the terms seem easy.

20

We hate small print.

Original problem:
announcement which says that I'm terrific.

Redefined:
announcement which says that if you don't know how
terrific I am, you damn well ought to.

**Bob Gill, formerly blah, blah, blah,
blah, blah, blah, blah, blah, blah, blah,
blah, blah, blah, blah, blah, blah and blah.
Founded blah, blah, blah, blah, blah,
blah, blah, blah, blah, blah, blah, blah, blah,
blah, blah, blah, blah, blah, blah and blah.
Awarded a blah, blah, blah, blah, blah,
blah, blah, blah, blah, blah, blah and blah.
He recently blah, blah, blah, blah, blah,
blah, blah, blah, blah, blah, blah, blah and
blah, blah, blah, blah, blah, blah, blah.
He then blah, blah, blah, blah, blah,
blah, blah and is now available for design
and advertising projects at One Fifth Ave.,
New York, NY 10003. Tel: 212 460 0950.**

Original problem:
name a cookbook of Jewish recipes and then design the jacket.

Redefined:
make a relationship between good recipes and being Jewish.

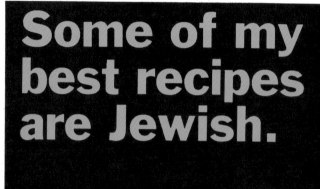

Original problem:
booklet cover to persuade mid-western, sports minded,
non-theatre goers to go to the theatre.

Redefined:
booklet cover which makes the most exaggerated claims
—and at the same time, doesn't take itself too seriously.

Live theatre is more exciting than television or movies or sports.

Well, maybe not sports.

People have been making images for the past eight
million years.

Images like x-rays, flags, NASA Moon photographs,
comic books, cave paintings, theatre masks, engineering
drawings, pub signs, graffiti, Civil War daguerreotypes,
engravings, Christmas cards, the Mona Lisa, etc.

These images, depending upon how they are used,
can transcend their original narrow purpose. They can
represent a period of history, or a cultural attitude. Or
they can symbolize very precise ideas.

If a designer finds one of these images (say, an engraving
of an Edwardian couple dancing) and it communicates
perfectly what he wants to say, why bother to invent a
new one? Why not use (steal) the engraving.

What makes a designer's work personal and original is
the *way* he uses images to communicate and to solve
problems. His ideas. Not necessarily the images
themselves. I didn't invent any of the images in this
section. They were all stolen. But, by using them in
a new context or by altering them in some way never
conceived of by their creators, I made them mine.

Original problem:
piano recital program cover.

Redefined:
piano recital program cover which illustrates that the
program ranges from Bach to Gershwin.

Original problem:
poster for an Edwardian comedy about divorce.

Redefined:
how can a non-visual idea such as *divorce* be made
visual?

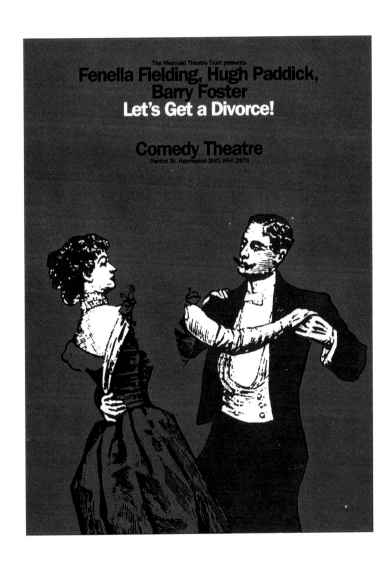

Original problem
logo for a real estate developer.

Redefined:
a logo for a real estate developer is too abstract—better
to think of a logo for someone who owns houses.

28

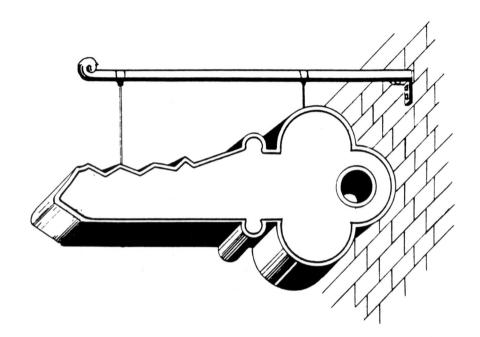

Original problem:
logo for a cinematographer

Redefined:
logo for someone with lots of equipment and who's available to go anywhere.

Original problem:
poster campaign for a newspaper to persuade people that
its classified advertising gets good results.

Redefined:
what do good classified advertising results look like?

30

EVENING STANDARD
for small ads
ring FLE 3000
NING STANDARD DAILY HOME FINDER
SOLD

The next time you see a sixteen color, blind embossed,
gold stamped, die cut, elaborately folded and bound job,
printed on hand made paper, see if it isn't a mediocre
idea trying to pass for something more.

There's a Chinese proverb which says that Nature uses as
little of anything as possible.

Me too.

Original problem:
ad for an advertising agency which promises never to do boring advertising.

Redefined:
how can boring advertising be presented in an exciting way?

34

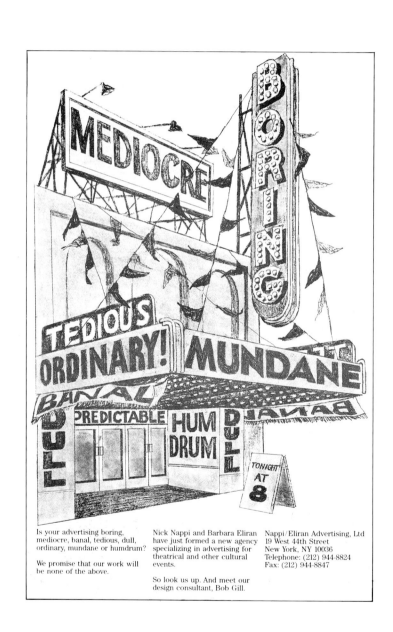

Is your advertising boring, mediocre, banal, tedious, dull, ordinary, mundane or humdrum?

We promise that our work will be none of the above.

Nick Nappi and Barbara Eliran have just formed a new agency specializing in advertising for theatrical and other cultural events.

So look us up. And meet our design consultant, Bob Gill.

Nappi/Eliran Advertising, Ltd
19 West 44th Street
New York, NY 10036
Telephone: (212) 944-8824
Fax: (212) 944-8847

Original problem:
illustration to represent a company on call twenty four
hours a day.

Redefined:
how can you recognize a company which is on call twenty
four hours a day?

Occasionally I write and illustrate children's books. *The Ups and the Downs* is about two communities, one at the top of a hill and the other, at the bottom. The Ups hate the Downs and their animals because they have huge

heads and tiny bodies. The Downs hate the Ups because they and their animals have tiny heads and huge bodies. But it all turns out right in the end, when they meet halfway and realize that they all look the same.

Original problem:
covers for booklets about a new advertising agency with
partners who have been in the business for many years.

Redefined:
how can you illustrate a new, old institution?

Original problem:
department store poster reminding their customers about
Mother's Day.

Redefined:
how can you say "Mother's Day" without saying
"Mother?"

40

Original problem:
cover for a magazine readership survey.

Redefined:
instead of showing a typical reader, why not a typical
non-reader?

Original problem:
ad for a film comedy about absolutely nothing but violence.

Redefined:
ad for a film comedy where every character is about to murder, or be murdered.

42

Original problem:
magazine illustration: portrait of a psychiatrist.

Redefined:
I'm not sure why I did what I did.

Original problem:
illustration: inexpensive day trips out of New York City.

Redefined:
make a relationship between *inexpensive* and *trips out of New York City.*

44

Original problem:
illustration: much more to a company than meets the eye.

Redefined:
much more to *anything* than meets the eye.

Designers are not usually very good copywriters. Most copywriters aren't much good, either. So, chances are that the words a designer has to deal with are not going to be very inspired.

If this is the case, then a designer is better off letting the graphics do all of the attention getting and letting the words give the information in the most straightforward way.

On the other hand, as I said in a previous section, if the words are attention getting, then the graphics should be straightforward.

The most important thing is to make sure that the words and the graphics never compete with each other.

Original problem:
logo for a comedy about a patient and his nurse.

Redefined:
how can a name look like it's the name of a patient?

HOROWITZ
& Mrs. Washington

Original problem:
logo for a United Nations Association luncheon.

Redefined:
logo for an institution which, usually, has boring
luncheons, but, which, this time might be different.

Original problem:
logo for BCM, a furniture manufacturer.

Redefined:
design letterforms inspired by the client's furniture.

The square, bold furniture suggested square, bold
letterforms. A logical, boring solution. Sometimes,
instead of trying another direction, I stay with an idea
which seems boring at first, but which *might* be pushed
further.

I tried making the square letterforms *more* like the
furniture by suggesting the third dimension.

Still, much too ordinary for a logo.

Finally, a unique version of a three-dimensional, square letterform, which I never would have discovered had I not played with the obvious.

Problem:
poster for a repertory theatre season.

Redefined:
poster for a historical play, a comedy, a fantasy, an adventure, a romance and a musical.

52

Original problem:
trade ad for *Nomads,* a film about teen age gangs.

Redefined:
how would the gang do the title, and where would they
do it?

Cinema 7 presents
Nomads starring Lesley Anne Down, Pierce Brosnan
Anna Jemison, Adam Ant, Josie Cotton, Frank Doubleday
Hector Mercado, Mary Woronov

Executive Producer: Jerry Gershwin
Produced by George Pappas & Cassian Elwes
Written & Directed by John McTiernan

Original problem:
logo for a film production with two partners.

Redefined:
logo for a film production company with one producer
multiplied by two.

Original problem:
cover for a fund raising booklet.

Redefined:
cover which makes a relationship between the name and
fundraising.

Original problem:
poster for a graphic design exhibition.

Redefined:
as graphic design is concerned with clear communication
(especially mine), I decided to be unclear, just to be
contrary.

Original problem:
logo for a film which will appeal to teenagers.

Redefined:
logo for a film which parents will hate.

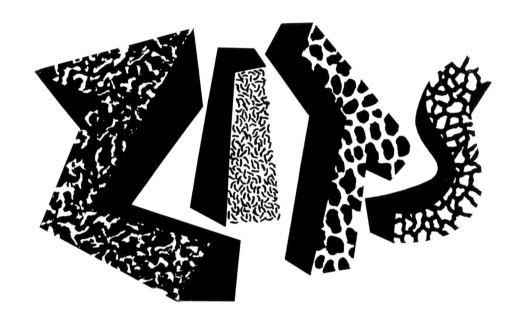

Original problem:
logo for a national chain of opticians.

Redefined:
how can a name extend from coast to coast?

Original problem:
logo for a theatrical version of *Alice*.

Redefined:
make a relationship between *Alice* and the looking glass.

ALICE IN
WONDERLAND

Original problem:
logo for investment counselors.

Redefined:
make a relationship between the name and finance.

I eventually decided to print all of the stationery and
business cards on safety paper, with a background
pattern usually seen on checks.

60

Original problem:
logo for a shopping center in a converted 100 year old factory.

Redefined:
logo for a Victorian shopping center.

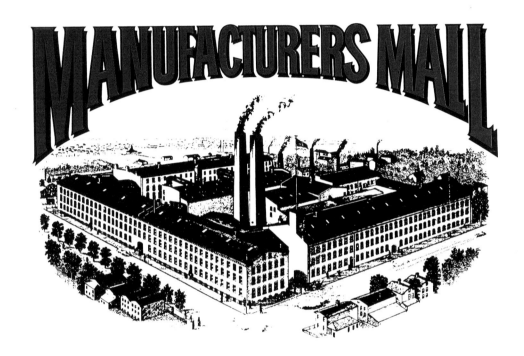

Skull and crossbones = pirate. Stars and stripes = America. A sunrise = a fresh start.

The good news is that the more common an image, the greater its potential as instant communication.

The bad news is that these common images are used so often that chances are they are no longer of any interest. However, if fresh ways can be found to present these images, they are almost guaranteed to be effective.

Original problem:
logo for special effects company which can put their
customers in any still photo or video.

Redefined:
logo which illustrates wish fulfillment.

64

Original problem:
birth announcement.

Redefined:
announcement of amazing, incredible, spectacular birth.

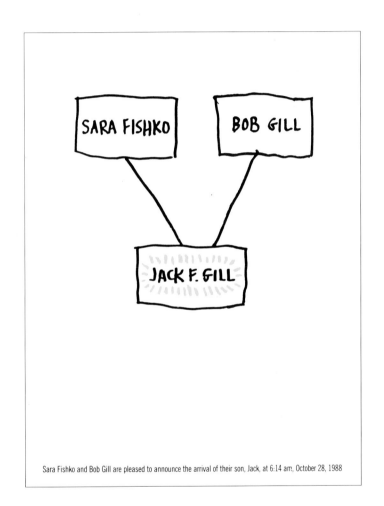

Sara Fishko and Bob Gill are pleased to announce the arrival of their son, Jack, at 6:14 am, October 28, 1988

Original problem:
logo for a film production company.

Redefined:
is it possible to do something fresh with the ultimate film cliché?

66

Original problem:
logo for a musical about how Hollywood corrupts a writer.

Redefined:
is it possible to do something fresh with the ultimate film cliché?

Original problem:
moving announcement.

Redefined:
moving announcement = change of address = new bell
= dymo type.

68

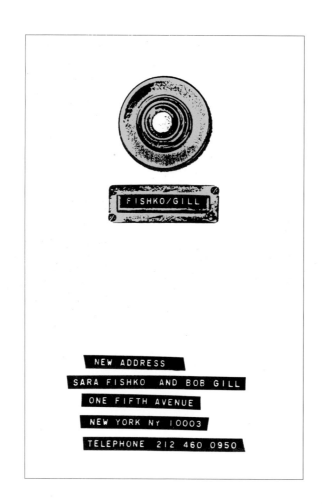

Original problem:
ad for various adult education courses.

Redefined:
make a relationship between giving up smoking, losing weight, racquet ball and tap dancing.

Consider the following three typical design jobs:

a jacket for a mystery about the murder of a clown,
a poster for a music festival in Wyoming,
an ad which says, "give oranges for Christmas."

Each job involves two unrelated subjects:

murder	clown
music	Wyoming
oranges	Christmas

This section is supposed to demonstrate that it should
always be possible to combine any two unrelated ideas
into *one* simple image, and that one simple image is
often the best way to communicate.

Original problem:
logo for a play about the personal triumph of a defeated
fighter.

Redefined:
find one simple image which relates a triumphant fighter
and a woman.

Original problem:
logo for a musical about a loser with an ironic title.

Redefined:
make a relationship between the ironic title and the loser.

Original problem:
illustration for a speedwriting course.

Redefined:
make a relationship between speed and writing.

Original problem:
illustration for a poetry appreciation course.

Redefined:
make a relationship between a book and poetry.

74

Original problem:
illustration for how to operate an office cleaning business.

Redefined:
make a relationship between cleaning and study.

Original problem:
illustration for how to tell the difference between junk and antiques.

Redefined:
make a relationship between antiques and junk.

Original problem:
airline snack package.

Redefined:
lighter than air package.

Original problem:
counter display for a slipper.

Redefined:
what can hold a slipper and be amusing at the same time?

Original problem:
moving announcement for an art gallery.

Redefined:
moving announcement for paintings.

**The Forum Gallery is moving to
745 Fifth Ave., New York, NY 10151 Tel: 212 355-4545   Fax: 212 355-4547
on December 1, 1991.**

Original problem:
logo for a company which makes beer, soft drinks and
various bottled waters.

Redefined:
what is the simplest image associated with beer, soft
drinks and bottled waters?

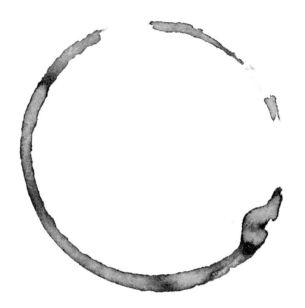

If the square didn't exist, we'd have to invent it.

The square, more than any other shape, represents
perfection. It also, for me, represents inevitability.
Perhaps that's why I find myself returning to the square
as the basis of a logotype, over and over again.

Original problem:
logo for Datascope Corp., manufacturers of intensive care
monitoring equipment.

Redefined:
put a *D* in a very precise environment.

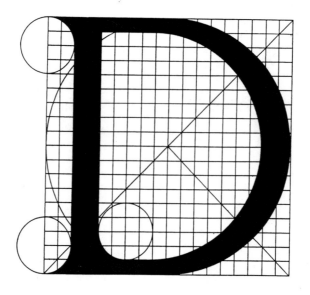

Original problem:
logo for Formation Furniture, specializing in modular
seating.

Redefined:
a modular logo.

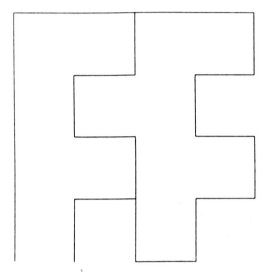

Original problem:
logo to represent British packaged goods at International
trade fairs.

Redefined:
make a relationship between Britain and packaged
goods.

84

Original problem:
logo for the Grill Room restaurant.

Redefined:
a grill is a natural logo. Do justice to it.

The most or the biggest or tallest *anything* is fascinating. If you're in any doubt, take a look in the Guinness Book of Records.

Who can fail to be overwhelmed by the cast of thousands in Leni Riefenstahl's *Triumph of the Will* or by a perfect scale model of the Eiffel Tower made out of 6,300,521 matchsticks by a retired locomotive driver?

What does any of this have to do with design?

Don't ever do anything in moderation. If the solution calls for a lot of color, then use more color than ever seen by anyone. If the type is supposed to be big, then let it be really big.

Take any idea or graphic direction as far as you can take it. And then, after you think you've taken it as far as you can, you'll find that you can take it further.

Remember, it's not natural to go to an extreme in anything. That's why I'm recommending it.

Original problem:
poster for a play about a father who goes berserk and
murders his son.

Redefined:
how can a *poster* go berserk?

Original problem:
magazine illustration of heavy traffic.

Redefined:
question: what is the ultimate image of heavy traffic?
Answer: when more than one car occupies the same space.

Original problem:
one month of a calendar.

Redefined:
one month = the passage of time.

(I hired a student to allow me to have him photographed
as more and more of his hair was cut off. Then, I
arranged the photographs in reverse order.)

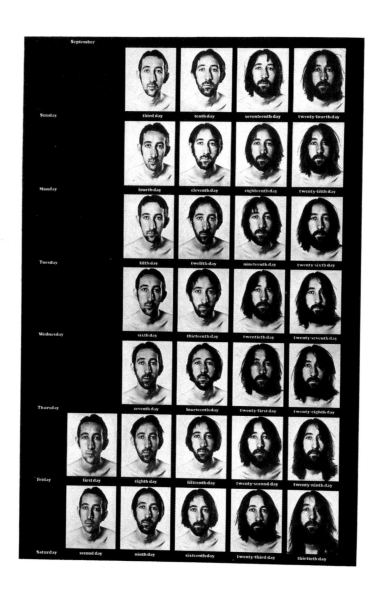

I keep changing, one of my children's books, is about
how a child's perception of the world keeps changing.

**Compared with Uncle Martin,
I seem to have so much hair...**

**but when he turns round,
I seem to have so little.**

Original problem:
annual report cover for an adult education company.

Redefined:
annual report cover for an adult education company with
branches in many cities.

Original problem:
annual report cover for adult education company.

Redefined:
annual report cover for an adult education company
which gives many courses.

The Learning Annex Annual Report: 1988

It is surprising the number of people, including artists
and designers, who still think of a portrait merely as a
likeness. (A map showing the locations of eyes, nose,
mouth, etc.)

I think a portrait must do much more than look like its
subject. It should have a point of view, an opinion about
its subject.

The opinion (statement) should come before any preconceptions about technique or style.

If the statement is interesting, then the portrait is more
likely to be interesting. *Listen* to the statement. It will tell
you if it is best done in black and white, or in gold leaf,
or day-glo, or in some other color(s).

It will also tell you if it should reveal the minutest detail
or be very simple. Realistic or decorative or abstract? If
abstract, then hard edge or not? If decorative, what sort
of decoration? Tantric, Medieval or any one of infinite
possibilities?

The next time you begin a portrait, wait a minute. Think
about what you want to say, or what you are feeling.

Original problem:
magazine cover: the president and the head of the
Federal Reserve can't agree on fiscal policy.

Redefined:
transform stock, neutral photographs into belligerent
images.

Original problem:
poster for a debate about contemporary values.

Redefined:
poster for a debate in which the combatants have
absolutely nothing in common. (Not even the illustration
technique.)

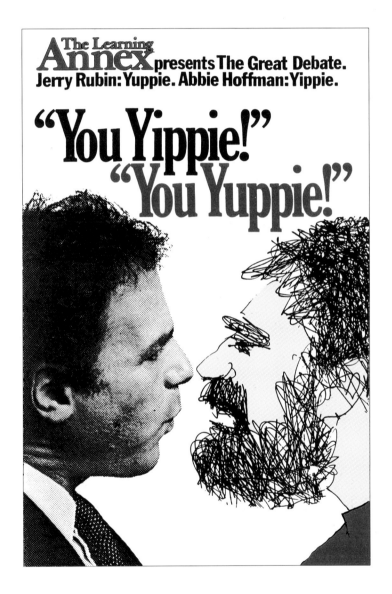

Albert Einstein

Original problem:
illustrations for an annual report of a corporation with
offices in New York and London

Redefined:
discover differences between New York and London
characters.

Original problem:
cover for a cassette of Bob and Ray radio shows.

Redefined:
translate Bob and Ray's dry radio humor into visual terms.

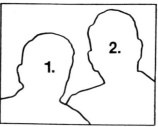

1. Bob   2. Ray

Original problem:
logo for a film about sexual undercurrents, *The Severed Head*.

Redefined:
logo for an orgy.

Original problem:
poster for a musical featuring two stars who are
guaranteed equal billing.

Redefined:
in order to achieve equal billing, put both stars in one
shape.

Original problem:
poster for a play about the Nazi occupation of Paris in
World War II.

Redefined:
find an image to dramatize the ironic title.

Original problem:
logo for *Local Stigmatic,* a black comedy film.

Redefined:
a black on black logo.

Original problem:
letterhead for a children's photographer.

Redefined:
how can a child's portrait be used on the letterhead
without interfering with the typing area?

Carole Cutner
portrait photography

6 Radnor Lodge
Sussex Pl London W2
tel: 723 7645

Original problem:
illustration for course on running a business at home.

Redefined:
how can you tell if someone's working at home?

108

Problem:
illustration for a course in how to get through to *anyone*
on the telephone.

Redefined:
illustration of the most difficult person in the world to get
through to on the telephone.

110

Original problem:
logo for a musical about Elvis.

Redefined:
logo for a shrine to Elvis.

Original problem:
logo for the film *Julius Caesar.*

Redefined:
how can you communicate that Caesar was once adored
and later destroyed in *one* image?

Original problem:
booklet to celebrate a theatre's twentieth anniversary.

Redefined:
a poster, suitable for framing, with some of the
distinguished playwrites whose work the theater has
presented in the past twenty years.

114

Some of the company our company's welcomed to Indiana since 1972.
Seated: L to R: T.S. Eliot, Somerset Maugham and Tennessee Williams. Standing: L to R: George Bernard Shaw, August Strindberg, Harold Pinter, Arthur Miller, Oscar Wilde, Charles Dickens, Neil Simon, Agatha Christie, Tom Stoppard, Anton Chekov, Thornton Wilder, William Shakespeare, Henrik Ibsen, Lillian Hellman and Noel Coward.
Produced for the friends of the Indiana Repertory Theatre on the occasion of their Twentieth Anniversary.

Original problem:
illustration for *Zits,* a teen age film about kids who get
themselves into trouble.

Redefined:
illustration for a film about five kids who find themselves
in hot water.

(It's about five kids who find themselves in hot water.)

Original problem:
poster for a film about a boy who runs back and forth
delivering the messages of two lovers.

Redefined:
how can the boy run in *both* directions at the same time?

116

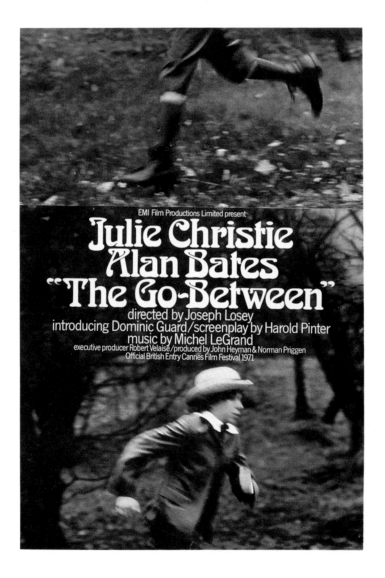

Illustration for the cover of *I keep changing,* one of my children's books.

The bird and the pig appear again inside the book.

My father thinks I eat like this.	My mother thinks I eat like this.

Original problem:
logo for a ballet about sexual stereotypes, *Dangerous Games.*

Redefined:
logo for a ballet which treats real people as if they were two dimensional.

Original problem:
logo for *Images*, a film about someone preoccupied with death and unable to tell reality from fantasy.

Redefined:
make a relationship between Susanna York and death.

122

Original problem:
logo for *Chorus of Disapproval,* a film about someone who
tries to seduce every woman he meets.

Redefined:
can you shore more than one seduction at a time?

Original problem:
poster for a rock musical which also has 5,000 years of multi-media imagery.

Redefined:
make a relationship between the present and the past.

124

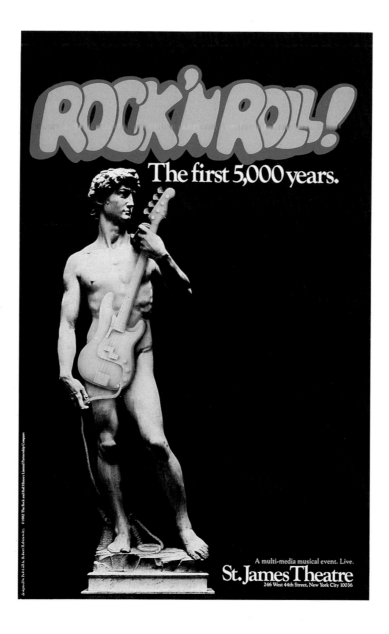

Original problem:
poster for a lecture and workshop on how designers can deal with difficult clients.

Redefined:
poster for a lecture and workshop on how Davids can deal with Goliaths.

Original problem:
illustration about how pipe smoking improves one's image.

Redefined:
make a distinguished image, and then take the pipe out of it.

126

Original problem:
illustration of a "light" cigarette.

Redefined:
illustration of a cigarette so light, that it defies gravity.

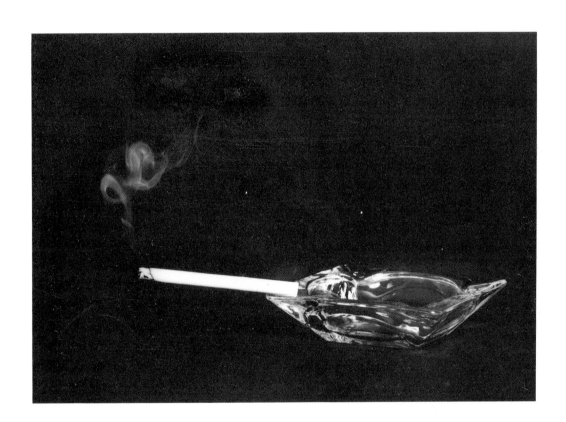

Original problem:
illustration to promote a singles dinner-dance.

Redefined:
cast the ideal Yuppie couple, and then photograph them
thirty-five times.

128

Original problem:
annual report cover for a film production company. The client requested that I show as much as possible of their most valuable asset.

Redefined:
show Raquel Welch an *infinite* number of times.

There are many myths in the design and advertising world. The one I find particularly dangerous is:

most graphic design and advertising is so predictable and vapid because of the dumb, Philistine clients.

That's what designers and agencies say. I say that getting one's best work *accepted* by clients is as much a part of the problem as solving the problem; that there's no such thing as a bad client—only a bad designer or a bad agency.

This section shows work which I couldn't get past the client.

When I am given a problem, although I often consider many solutions, I *never* show more than one idea at a time to the client. That is not to say that it is perfect, only that it is the *best* idea up until that moment. If it is rejected, I take note of the criticism and go away and think again. This usually results in a *better* idea than the original one. Even when the criticism is arbitrary, it has been my experience that it always contains a grain of useful information, or at least something to stimulate a fresh look at the problem.

Too many designers and agencies show their clients not one, or even a number of their best ideas, but any scrap of paper that has the remotest chance of being liked— regardless of its quality.

No wonder we're drowning in banal images. It's our own fault. Not the client's.

I was asked to design a poster for a very literary comedy set in the eighteenth century, about a pompous, know-it-all.

My first solution (a clown) was rejected. So was my second (an ass). And my third. And my fourth, which I thought was my best.

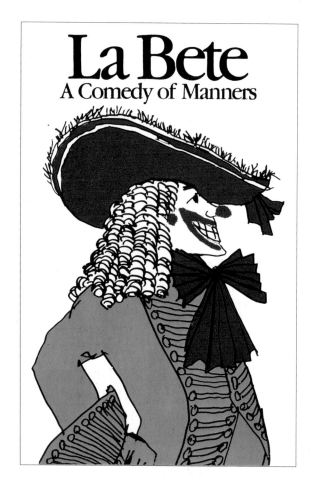

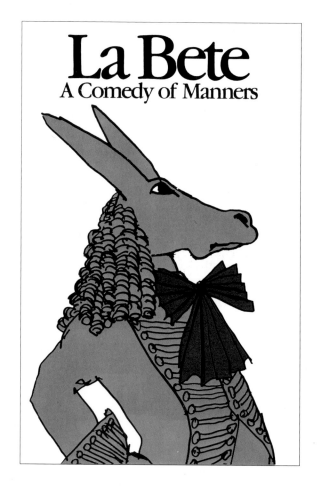

(The Schmuck)

Here are two solutions to the same problem.

I decided that rather than try and illustrate the bizarre details of the plot—I could best serve this comedy about love, by limiting myself to the most obvious symbol of love, while at the same time, communicating that this play was not your usual sitcom.

134

The producer eventually went with a conventional
photograph of the two stars.

The Indiana Repertory Theatre asked me to design a logo. They suggested that I use their initials. I agreed, and tried to make a relationship between IRT and the theatre.

I presented the back of a piece of scenery with their initials stenciled on it. They rejected it saying that they *never* use flats. Flats are for amateur theatre clubs.

The next three presentations were equally disastrous.

136

Too amateurish.

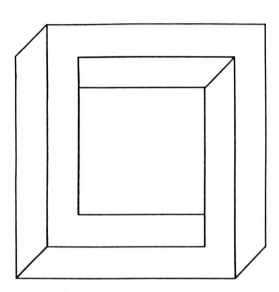

Too modern.

Too glamorous.

Too dramatic.

(I'm still working on it.)

The original problem was to show a range of paper samples. Designers and other specifiers of paper are usually sent quite elaborate mailers by paper mills. These promotions attract attention for a moment or two, and then disappear into a file, or a waste paper basket.

I suggested that a desk diary, with a double page spread for each week, would be a good vehicle to show paper samples with various printing possibilities; that if it were interesting, people might actually *use* it every day, for a year.

As each spread would be seen for a week, I tried to give more than interesting graphics. My solution was to collect pairs of wise sayings which contradicted each other, or a wise saying which contradicted itself, and illustrate the paradoxical words with a paradoxical image.

139

"Why climb a mountain? Because it's there."
George Mallery

"Why do writers write? Because it isn't there."
Thomas Berger

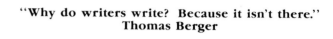

"Some things have to be seen to be believed."
S. Harward

"Some things have to be believed to be seen."
Ralf Hodgson

**"Whom the Gods would destroy,
they first make mad." Euripides**

**"Whom the Gods would destroy,
they first call promising." Cyril Connelly**

"The grass is always greener   on the other side of the fence."   Erasmus

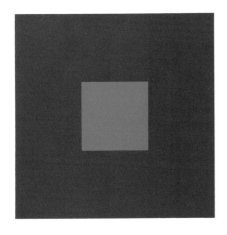

"Capitalism is the exploitation of man by man.   Communism is the reverse."   Polish joke

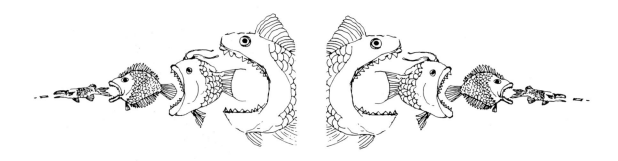

''News is the same thing happening every day   to different people.'' Anon.

"Every woman should marry — and no man."
Benjamin Disraeli

"All women marry beneath them."   Nancy Lady Astor

"A fool is a fool forever."   **Yiddish proverb**

"When the majority's wrong, the majority's right."
Pierre Claude Nivelle delaChaussee

Occasionally, in the course of working on a conventional problem, I stumble upon a solution which suggests a new format or a new technique of communication.

I only wish it happened more often.

Original problem:
poster for a kitch, fifties musical

Redefined:
is it possible to design a very corny image, as if the cast
did it themselves, and, at the same time, a sophisticated
poster?

Solution:
design an amateurish leaflet, xerox it on cheap paper...

put the leaflet under the windshield wiper of a fifties convertible, and photograph it.

I also suggested that, to compliment the posters, the producer xerox 10,000 leaflets, and have them put under the windshield wipers of every car within a few miles of the theatre.

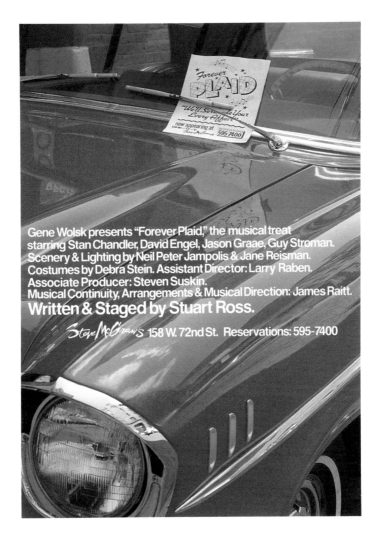

Original problem:
business card and mailer for a modest studio which does
design, typesetting, mechanicals and photostats.

Redefined:
make something special out of the modest services.

Instead of one business card, why not four business
cards, accordion folded?

152

A. JAIME

JAIME ASSOCIATES
STANDARD GRAPHIC DESIGN

527 MADISON AVENUE
NEW YORK CITY 10022   (212) 832-9047

A. JAIME

JAIME ASSOCIATES
THE USUAL TYPESETTING

527 MADISON AVENUE
NEW YORK CITY 10022   (212) 832-9047

A. JAIME

JAIME ASSOCIATES
VERY ORDINARY PHOTOSTATS

527 MADISON AVENUE
NEW YORK CITY 10022   (212) 832-9047

A. JAIME

JAIME ASSOCIATES
AVERAGE PASTE-UP & MECHANICALS

527 MADISON AVENUE
NEW YORK CITY 10022   (212) 832-9047

The most interesting thing about us is that we design, set the type, shoot the stats and do the mechanicals all in the same place. This means that there are no outside suppliers to prevent us from delivering your job on time. So, if you're planning a newsletter or a brochure or a slide presentation or any other printed matter, please think of us.

Jaime Associates: 527 Madison Avenue, New York City 10022 (212) 832-9047

Original problem:
poster to persuade as many Americans as possible to listen to an important radio discussion.

Redefined:
represent (involve) as many Americans as possible.

Solution:
represent an *infinite* number of Americans. I designed the poster to be trimmed in two ways. *A:* the top 23″, which includes the headline. *B:* the bottom 23″, which excludes the headline, but which includes three additional rows of heads.

154

The two versions of the poster (one with the headline, one without) are now the same size. When they are put together, it appears that the heads on each are different; that they are two totally different images.

One *A* poster, together with any number of *B* posters can now fill any space of any proportion. The final result, hopefully, comes as close as possible to representing an infinite number of Americans.

Index

Client/Publisher	Description	Collaborators	Date	Page
Fucci-Stone Prods.	Logo	drawing: Bobby Gill	1970	54
Geers/Gross Adv.	Illustrations: annual report		1986	100/101
Bob Gill	Announcement: Blah, blah…		1990	21
Jack Gill	Birth announcement		1988	65
Great Neck Theatre	Illustration: *House of Bernarda Alba*		1956	110
Grey Entertainment	Posters: *La Bête*		1990	132/133
Grey Entertainment	Posters: *The Sum of Us*		1990	134/135
Grill Room	Logo		1988	85
Hemdale Ltd.	Logo: *Images*	photo: John Summerhayes	1974	122
Imagine Yourself, Inc.	Logo		1989	64
Indiana Repertory Theatre	Logos		1991	136/137
Indiana Repertory Theatre	Booklet cover: 1991–92 Season		1991	22
Indiana Repertory Theatre	Booklet cover: can		1991	55
Indiana Repertory Theatre	Poster: 1991–92 Season		1991	52
Indiana Repertory Theatre	Poster: 20th anniversary		1991	114
Al Jaime	Business card, poster		1981	152/153
Elliott Kastner	Logo: *The Severed Head*	photo: John Summerhayes	1977	103
Elliott Kastner	Trade ad: *Nomads*	photo: Marty Jacobs retoucher: Sol Schnaer	1984	53
Elliott Kastner	Trade ad: *The Mummy of Canal Street*		1988	42
Elliott Kastner	Logo: *Zits*		1988	57
Elliott Kastner	Illustration: *Zits*		1988	115
Elliott Kastner	Booklet Cover: *Local Stigmatic*	photo: Marty Jacobs	1988	106
Elliott Kastner	Logo: *Chorus of Disapproval*	photo: John Alp	1988	123
The Learning Annex	Ad: Yippie/Yuppie	photo: Marty Jacobs	1987	97
The Learning Annex	Small ad: before/after		1987	69
The Learning Annex	Illustration: subway	photo: Marty Jacobs	1987	44
The Learning Annex	Illustration: the Queen	photo: unknown	1988	109
The Learning Annex	Booklet covers: annual reports	photos: Marty Jacobs	1987/ 1988	92/93
The Learning Annex	Illustration: yuppie dance	photo: Marty Jacobs retoucher: Sol Schnaer	1989	128
The Learning Annex	Spot illustrations		1989	74/75
The Learning Annex	Booklet cover: Hell's Angels	photo: Marty Jacobs	1989	41
The Learning Annex	Illustration: Einstein		1990	99
The Learning Annex	Illustration: working at home		1990	108
Martins RentaCar	Booklet cover: small print		1970	20
Mermaid Theatre Trust	Poster: *Let's Get a Divorce*		1969	27

160

Bob Gill is a designer, an illustrator, a copywriter, a teacher, a film-maker, and a terrible jazz pianist.

He went to London on a whim in 1960 and stayed 15 years. He started Fletcher/Forbes/Gill, a design office with the two brightest designers in England. F/F/G began with two assistants and a secretary. Today, it's called Pentagram, with offices everywhere except Albania.

Gill resigned in 1967 to work independently in London. He returned to New York in 1975 to write and design *Beatlemania,* the largest multi-media musical ever on Broadway, with Robert Rabinowitz, the painter.

Forget all the rules you ever learned about graphic design. Including the ones in this book. was published in 1981. It soon became required reading in design classes around the world.

Gill is still working independently, and still teaching. He recently had a one-man show at the Museum of Images and Sound in São Paulo, and was elected to the New York Art Director's Club Hall of Fame. This is his fourteenth book.

He's now living in New York with his wife, Sara Fishko, a film editor and radio producer, their three year old son, Jack, and their newborn daughter, Kate.